Aparna Karthikeyan is a dog mother, tree hugger and story teller. She has written for newspapers and websites about culture and livelihoods; books for big people (*Nine Rupees an Hour*, about the disappearing livelihoods of Tamil Nadu), and for children *Kali Wants to Dance* and *Cat's Egg*. She shares her home with her husband, daughter, plenty of books, and two very important creatures—her dogs Puchu and Shingmo.

Aparna Karthikeyan

Illustrated by
Sagar Kolwankar

First published by Red Panda, an imprint of Westland Publications Private Limited, in 2020

1st Floor, A Block, East Wing, Plot No. 40, SP Infocity, Dr MGR Salai, Perungudi, Kandanchavadi, Chennai 600096

Westland, the Westland logo, Red Panda and the Red Panda logo are the trademarks of Westland Publications Private Limited, or its affiliates.

Copyright © Aparna Karthikeyan, 2020

ISBN: 9789395767194

All rights reserved
Book design by New Media Line Creations, New Delhi 110 062

Printed at Nutech Print Services - India, Faridabad

Contents

SHINGMO, THE HEROINE
Trusting, affectionate, clumsy, lovable
THUG, HEAD OF THE DISREPUTABLES
Fearless, spiteful, misunderstood
MINE!!
PUCHU, THE BIG-SISTER
Caring, protective, smart, eager to please
MOM
LOLA, THE THREE-LEGGED SPRINTER
Spirited, swift, sporting
SWOOSHH...

THE TWINS (BABY DIANE AND FAT BROTHER)
Goofy, hungry, adventurous
MINE!
DUSTBIN IS BEST
CHIPS
THIN, THE FOSTER-MOTHER
Kind, noble, loyal, simple
HMM.
COCONUT, THE BEACH ELDER
Wise, compassionate, gentle
KRYA, THE DON
Feisty, dominating, brave, born leader

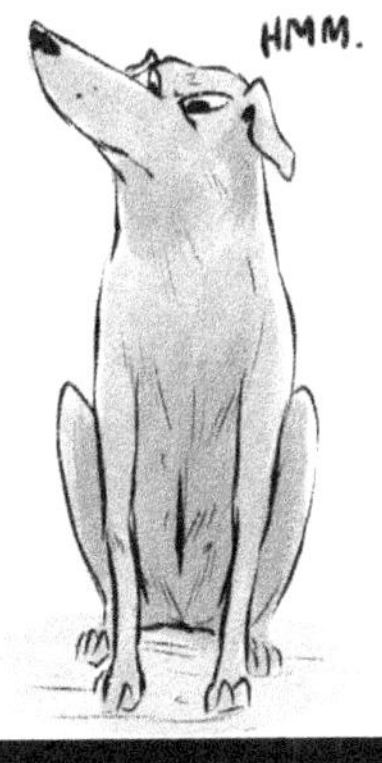

CHAPTER ONE

A New Pup on the Block

On the third day of the great Mumbai monsoon, a small cardboard box appeared on the beach. It had rained and rained all afternoon; the sky was still and grey, and the sand was soggy. The box got wet very quickly. It started wriggling. The jute rope around its middle danced; the packaging tape along its sides bulged. Suddenly, a leg punched a hole through the top; quickly, another popped out. Then came a very long nose. And one folded ear. By the time half the creature had emerged, a small crowd had gathered. They were all dogs. And they were not happy.

'Who is this?' asked Big Head. He was tall and brown, with a large forehead.

'It's a mouse,' Orange said, 'and it's ugly.'

'I don't think so,' Chocolate said, shaking her beautiful silky head. 'It sounds odd, very odd. I've heard this sound before ... in the market, I think.' She tilted her head when the creature cried again. 'It's a baby buffalo ...'

It began to drizzle.

The creature shivered, licked its lips nervously, and yawned anxiously.

'Actually,' Big Head said, 'it's a puppy ...'

'Don't be silly,' Orange said, 'puppies are cute. Like me. I'm very cute ...'

'You're just vain,' Chocolate snapped. 'Look, the sky is getting dark. We need to do something about this ... animal ... go bring Krya.'

Orange jumped when he heard the name. 'Why me? She'll box my ears if I disturb her!'

'Big Head, you go then,' Chocolate ordered.

'No, thank you,' Big Head replied. 'Let her find it tomorrow.'

'She'll be very mad at us if we don't—' Chocolate began arguing, but stopped.

Krya was already there. She had crept up behind them and was inspecting the animal, smelling it carefully from nose to tail. The creature trembled, crouching deep inside the cardboard box, shrinking its head and legs and whimpering.

'Who dumped this here?' Krya growled, poking the animal's head. It peed in fright.

Big Head, Chocolate and Orange took a step back. Their tails fell, their ears drooped, and they looked at their paws.

'We, we ...' Big Head stammered, 'we didn't see ...'

'Right. Your eyes and ears are only for decoration,' Krya snarled. Her fur caught the pale, fading light. It turned gold; it shimmered. 'You don't see and you don't hear ... and during your watch, someone abandons one more sick puppy on the beach.'

The dogs hung their heads, ashamed.

Krya looked inside the box—it still trembled, and sad, hiccupping sounds came from within. 'It's quite ill. I don't think it will make it. Chocolate, keep an eye,' she snapped. 'I'm going to check on Coconut; he's sick too,' she said, and walked away, turning back once to look at the box that was now moving backwards, slowly, slowly, until it was next to the workmen's cabin.

'Every day,' Krya muttered, 'every single day, some creature is dumped on the beach. Do those people know how ridiculously hard it is to survive here?'

She wasn't waiting for an answer. She knew it herself.

She had landed up on the beach six years ago, on a bike, with a jute rope around her neck, and her

boy—who had carried her home in his lunch bag when he had found her alone outside his school—had hugged her one last time.

'Sorry, puppy,' he had told her. 'Daddy says I can't keep you; mummy says you'll bite me ... sorry, puppy.' He squeezed her hard. 'They said you'll find food here,' he went away, crying loudly.

And she did find food, eventually. In the beginning, there were only scraps that nobody wanted, not even the crows, and she was always hungry, always thirsty, but then she learnt how to beg from the people who came to the beach in the evenings and ate plates of pav bhaji and bhel puri and dosa. They gave her a morsel or two if she stared at them silently, looking hungry and sad (which she was), and after they left, she licked the plates and napkins, because there always was a tidbit or two stuck on them. She learnt to hang around the food stalls, the idli sellers' bicycles, the kulfi man's basket. She always wagged her tail and greeted them happily—and she truly was happy to see them—every day.

Soon she made friends with the resident pack of dogs, quickly becoming their leader, the Don. They all listened to her, because if they didn't, she flipped them over—even the ones taller and stouter—and stood over them. The next time they saw Krya, they obediently lay down, showed her their bellies, and wagged their tails.

Now she walked, her head high, her neck twisting this way and that, checking on the people, the dogs, the trees, the white-lipped waves, until she reached the spot where Coconut always slept.

There was a depression in the sand, but he wasn't there.

Where has he gone in this weather? Krya wondered. She could smell a storm—surely it wasn't far away. As if they agreed, the coconut trees above tossed their heads, the wind howled, the waves rose and crashed, a great bolt of lightning ran across the sky, and suddenly, for a second, the evening turned white. And from the sea, an old grey dog emerged ...

'Oh hullo, Krya,' Coconut said. 'What brings you here?'

'You fool!' Krya barked. 'I thought you were shivering with fever, and you're having a bath?'

'Is that what you thought I was doing?' Coconut shook his head, body and tail, and water flew everywhere; little droplets fell into the sand and disappeared.

'I can't think of any other reason you would come out of the sea,' Krya scoffed. She was angry and, by now, exhausted. She was upset about the new puppy; she was worried about Coconut—maybe, she thought, he was losing his mind.

'I went to give something back to the sea, Krya,' Coconut said, now circling the sand, beating it with his feet, curling up into a ball. 'There was a fish— it came in with the tide and got stuck in the mud. The crows wanted it for dinner, but it looked sad, so I took it in my mouth and dropped it off over there ...'

'Are you sure you didn't eat it yourself?' Krya asked, her eyes narrowing.

'I'm the Elder, Krya. Why would I lie?'

'Well, because...' Krya began, a little embarrassed.

'Never trust anyone, do you?' Coconut asked, closing his eyes, sighing, ready to sleep.

'Stubborn dog!' Krya muttered after she watched over him for a few minutes. 'He won't come to the shops and stay dry even in the worst of storms. And he says I don't listen to people ...'

'I heard you,' Coconut said. 'I'm fine here, Krya; you go and mind the new pup. We can't let another one die, can we?'

'Another? Who else died? Coconut, tell me,' Krya said.

But Coconut was asleep, and he wouldn't speak, not even when she poked his shoulder with her paw, so she went back to her spot behind the street lamp, the cement pillar offering a little shelter from the wind and rain, and she rolled herself into a tight ball, flipped her tail over her nose and slept ...

CHAPTER TWO

A Noble Beast

When the new pup woke up the next morning, the sun was bright, the air was warm and moist, and a giant shadow loomed over her. She looked up, saw a large tummy, a small tail and a friendly nose.

'So you are the new puppy!' the dog woofed and wagged her tail.

The new puppy got up quickly, took three steps backwards, bumped into her box, peed next to it and shivered.

The dog shuffled forward. Her fur was everyday brown; her eyes were especially kind. She licked the puppy's head. 'You're a strange creature. Such a long nose, such a long tail and such floppy black ears. There, there. Don't be scared,' she said gently. 'I won't eat you ...'

The puppy trembled some more.

The brown dog continued licking her head. She licked her ears and nose and neck.

'Come with me,' the dog said. 'Let's find you something to eat.'

The puppy shook her small head.

'Trust me, you don't know how hungry you are ...' the dog said, and walked in front of the pup. The puppy followed. The dog stopped next to a large green dustbin overflowing with garbage.

'We're just in time,' the dog said, smacking her lips. 'In half an hour, the cleaning crew will empty all of this and take it away. They don't know the value of this fine buffet!' She shook her head sadly, then carefully sifted through the heap. 'Hmm, let's see what we have today. There is vada pav, some bread omelette, one poori and a little biriyani. What would you like, please?' the dog enquired politely, and began eating.

The puppy's tummy rumbled at the sight of all the food.

She grabbed the omelette from the dog's mouth. She gulped it down. She ate two bites of the vada pav and half a poori. And two minutes later, she vomited all of it.

'I feel sick!' the puppy moaned.

The next minute the dog was on her back and Krya was standing over her.

'Thin!' Krya yelled, 'I told you to see if it's alive, not kill it! How can you feed it this rubbish?'

'She looked hungry'—Thin wriggled under Krya's paws—'and I thought she might be stronger if …'

'Wait,' Krya said, getting off Thin. 'It's a girl? Come here, puppy. Lie down for your inspection …' And she gently flipped the shivering puppy and checked her. 'Hmm, you're right, Thin, and it's a good thing too. The boys won't think she's a threat …' Krya said. The puppy went and hid under Thin. 'Will you mind her?'

'Of course,' Thin said, 'of course. She's a sweet thing. I'll take her to my man—he'll come tomorrow—I'm sure he'll bring her medicines. She'll be okay, then she'll be my friend …'

'Stop dreaming, Thin,' Krya said. 'Let's wait for a few days, shall we?'

And with that, Krya stalked off. She had a lot of work in the mornings. She had to check if there were intruders in her territory. She had to meet the old uncle who gave her a belly rub and the policeman who patted her head and gave her three biscuits dipped in tea.

After she had gone far away, the puppy whispered, 'What is Thin?'

Thin replied, blushing, 'That's my name. I used to be thin, but now I'm a little fat, but I plan to go on a diet and—'

The puppy interrupted, 'What's a diet?'

Thin said, 'Ah, you know nothing! But you're in good hands—I will teach you everything. Now follow me for the grand tour …'

Thin took the puppy with her around the beach. She showed her the sea and the sky and the sun; where the sand was fine and warm; where she could sleep in the mornings. She told her when the sun rose over the buildings and trees, and where she could watch the sunset in the evenings.

'It happens every day,' Thin said, 'but people act like they've never seen it before!'

Next, Thin showed her the hotels, which marked the end of their territory.

'You go past that gate, that's the Bad Side—and those dogs will get you,' Thin warned. 'The pack on the other side is a little friendlier—that's the Good Side, because the dogs there are too old or too young to care. Oh, and remember, if a new dog or a big dog chases you, run into the water. It's safest there!'

The puppy was running behind Thin now. She was out of breath and tired.

'Thin, I want to sleep,' she said, and sat down quietly on the sand.

'Oh dear, come with me,' Thin said, and nudged the puppy gently with her snout.

The two walked on, the puppy stumbling behind Thin, until they reached a dry patch, next to a compound wall turned pink with fallen bougainvillea flowers. Three dogs were curled up in a row.

'This is where we sleep. You've met these three already, haven't you? They're our pack: Big Head, Orange and Chocolate. Our leader, the Don, is Krya. You must always obey her—if not, you're dead. Those are the shops—in the evenings they are filled with humans. Some are nice. Most don't mind dogs. A few hate us. If you see them lifting their hand suddenly and throwing something at you, RUN!'

The puppy was no longer listening. Her head drooped, her eyes closed and she lay down heavily on the sand. She slept.

CHAPTER THREE

Shingmo the Seventh

So you found yourself a baby! Thin's man lifted the new pup by her armpits and held her up. The puppy dangled from his hands, a reddish-brown thing. She wriggled her legs, twisting her face and nose and tail, until she shook herself free.

'What shall we call you? Snake? You're very slithery. But no, people will be scared of you then ... let's call you ... Shingmo!' And he kissed her nose. From his shirt pocket, he removed a small paper cover and carefully picked one red and one yellow tablet. Catching the puppy, he opened her mouth, placed the medicines on one side, clamped her jaws shut with one hand and stroked her throat with the other.

She swallowed the tablets.

'There, Shingmo. Soon your fever will be gone, and you won't be so pukey then. You might even grow to be like your friend!' He laughed and pulled Thin's plump cheeks from side to side. 'And there's not much time,' he said, shading his eyes with a hand and looking into the sunny horizon. 'The rain will be back again, and they say it will be very heavy and there will be flooding, and who knows when it will stop!'

'You're talking to the dogs again, Damu?' a voice called out, and Thin's man—his name was, yes, Damu—laughed and went to see his friend Gautam.

'There's a new puppy, and Thin has adopted her,' he told Gautam, and asked him for a cup of tea. 'Put it in my account; I have no money—I had to buy medicines for the dogs ...'

'If it's not medicines, you're buying them food. You're a fool, Damu, that's what you are,' Gautam teased him. 'So, what have you named that thing? And do you think it will survive?'

'She's a beauty. I hope she will. I'm calling her Shingmo,' Damu said, sipping his tea and watching the pack sitting around the puppy. 'It's as if they're talking to her, isn't it?'

'You talk so much nonsense, Damu, you should write story books.' Gautam punched his friend's arm.

Except it wasn't the stuff of storybooks at all. The dogs were indeed talking to Shingmo. Firstly, they congratulated her for a fine new name. Then they teased her about it.

'What is a Shingmo?' they asked her, laughing.

'How is she to know? She's tiny. Maybe that's what it means,' Thin said protectively.

'I am tiny,' Shingmo said. 'That's what my mother called me. She said I was the last puppy, the seventh one, and she was sure I was going to die ...'

'That explains why you're so sickly!' Big Head said. 'I was the first one. That's why I'm so strong!'

'You're a greedy pig—that's why you have such a big head,' Chocolate said. 'Be kind to the little one, won't you? Plus you're going to babysit her for a bit. Thin and I have some important business.'

'What do you want me to do? I can't play with small things. What if I break her or something?' Big Head asked, looking alarmed. 'Plus, what is this business? You two keep wandering everyday— Where do you go? Tell me!'

'Shan't,' Chocolate said, and Thin shook her head from side to side, and they gave the boys—and Shingmo—the slip and scooted.

Big Head and Orange looked at each other.

'We're in charge,' they said. 'Let's take Shingmo for a walk before Krya shouts at us.'

And so they did, asking the puppy to keep close. They went to the Good Side, where the trees swayed gently and threw beautiful, moving shadows on the ground.

'See that grey lump over there?' Big Head asked. 'That's Coconut. He's the beach Elder— he'll bore you with his stories about the olden days and a time when there was no crowd on Saturdays. Avoid him!'

'But why!' Orange asked. 'I love his stories. They're fun! Shingmo, I think you should talk to him!'

'Bah! Stupid advice. Next you'll be telling her to make friends with those two.' Big Head pointed at a couple of dogs running towards them.

'Why not?' Shingmo asked, tilting her head. 'Aren't they nice?'

'Over-friendly!' Orange said.

'Chatterboxes!' Big Head said.

'Nosey!' Orange said.

'Ravenous!' Big Head said.

The two dogs had reached them by then. They were short and stout and golden-brown. They looked like twins and spoke at the same time.

'What's your name?' they both asked, and before Shingmo could reply, they announced together that they were Baby Diane and Fat Brother.

'You can't tell who is who, and that's part of the fun,' they giggled.

'Hullo,' Shingmo said shyly, when they paused to catch their breath. 'My name's Shingmo. I'm new, and these two are taking me on a tour.'

'Wonderful! Is there a nap in your tour?' Baby Diane and Fat Brother asked. 'Because it's siesta time now, and if you just dig a little bit, you'll find some cool sand. And with the sun to warm your back,

you'll be in heaven! What's better, you might find a crumb or two—although that's hard to expect as we're very good at our jobs; we eat every morsel on our beach. If you do, please tuck in, and we'll even tell you a story while you fall asleep. Shall we tell her our story? I think we should. Some people thought we were Labradors and took us home, but we didn't know how to be Labradors, so they brought us to the beach and left us here. Coconut found us and taught us to be good beach dogs and that's what we are ...'

But by then, the others had fallen asleep, and so the brother and sister duo—who didn't know how to be Labradors—also slept. And that's exactly where Krya found them an hour later—five dogs, curled up like doughnuts, snoring gently, musically, next to a friendly sea ...

CHAPTER FOUR

A Wave So High ...

It rained and rained from a very black sky for two days.

They had never seen such rain, the dogs said. They sat, huddled, in the little passages between the shops. Krya had dragged Coconut with her when she saw the waves swallow the beach. Baby Diane and Fat Brother had come with her too. The dogs sat quietly, or slept in a heap, and every time it looked like it might stop raining, they ran out. But the rain came back fiercely, whipping their faces and backs, and they rushed back to their shelter.

At least, Coconut said, the shops were dry.

'So is my mouth,' said Fat Brother. Coconut told him to lick some of the rain water.

'Shingmo,' Coconut ordered, 'you come here and sit next to me.' The oldest and the youngest sat side by side, while Krya and Big Head watched the waves anxiously.

'Do you think the water will come in?' Orange asked, when the next wave crashed on the steps.

'Do you think this roof will fall?' Chocolate asked, when the wind tore at the awning, shredding it, and playing with the strips of red and yellow.

'Will Damu come?' Thin asked.

Nobody answered.

But everybody knew—people would not come to the beach, and even if they tried, the police would stop them.

And the dogs were not going to find any food …

By the third day, the dogs were exhausted. The cold, the wind, the rain, the hunger, all of it tormented them. They were scared and tired of sitting up and watching the drama: the furious rain, the angry waves, the boiling sea, the roaring wind, the trees that came crashing down, the water that took back, like a trophy, everything that it could find—rubbish bins, tyres, a bicycle, half a coconut tree, three push carts, plastic bottles, glass bottles, dead animals …

And they were worried Shingmo and Coconut would die too. Both were shivering; Shingmo's teeth were chattering. The puppy was not able to stand,

and when Thin nudged her with her snout, she made baby animal sounds and fell on the floor. Krya shook her head sadly when she saw the pup. She turned her face away, looked out over the sea ... and in the distance, above the horizon, she saw a little light.

Maybe, she thought, maybe the rain would end soon.

The last hour was the hardest; the dogs were very impatient, but Krya told them to wait until the rain stopped fully. Finally, when it did, the sun came out—a weak sun and watery sunshine—and they walked slowly to the beach ...

They could barely see the sand. It was covered with tons and tons of plastic and rubbish. Everything the sea had eaten and had been forced to eat, it had spat back; all that was pumped in from the city's gutters and sewers had been duly returned.

People came back to the beach slowly, one by one, and they looked disgusted. The shops remained closed. Damu was nowhere to be seen ...

Thin fretted over Shingmo. She was barely conscious.

Krya fretted over Coconut. His cough was terrible: a great hacking, followed by a dreadful gagging, and then a horrible wheezing.

But just when the dogs thought they were finished, a van came to the beach, and a lady walked towards them with a big packet in her hand. She placed some bowls on the ground and gave them all a warm meal of chicken and rice.

The dogs ate and ate, and when they were done, Fat Brother licked the lady's hands, Orange leapt on her, and Thin pulled at her kurta and tugged and tugged.

The lady understood.

'Where do you want me to come?' she asked, and followed Thin, who ran to the passage. When she saw Shingmo and Coconut, she said, 'oh no, oh no', and she ran to the van and brought the driver with her. Together, they carried both of them away …

This rain, the dogs thought sadly, had taken two of their friends.

But the lady brought them back that evening.

The sky was pale and purple, the sea gentle and calm, and somewhere on the east, a full moon rose and climbed up to sit with the stars.

And on that cool, clear June night, Coconut and Shingmo came back, wearing bandages on their front paws, where they were poked with needles. They were weak but happy to be home, and the puppy ran straight to Thin and licked her mouth. Thin washed Shingmo's face and back and tail, over and over.

'What happened, what happened?' The dogs crowded around the two.

Coconut coughed a little, but he slowly spoke, telling them about the doctor's clinic—tubes which dripped saline water; a special meal for very sick dogs that didn't taste very good, but which the doctors had made him eat; and injections of medicines and vitamins for both of them.

'And now I'm going to lie down under my tree,' he said, but Krya barked at him.

Her tone was so ferocious, he sat down quickly and listened to her. 'The lady will come looking for you tomorrow; I am sure you need more medicines. How will you get better if you run and hide?' Krya scolded. And stunned at being spoken to in that fashion, Coconut lay down obediently, and for a week, he followed Krya around like a puppy.

Many things happened in that week.

The cleaning crew worked night and day and day and night and took away truckloads of rubbish. The men and women who came in neon-coloured vests barely stood up straight; they spent whole mornings bending, picking up baskets and baskets of rubbish and chucking them into a tractor, which then tipped it all into the garbage lorry.

Slowly, the sand became visible. The sun shone again, the sea glinted, and the sky turned a beautiful blue. The trees were lush and green, and birds sang in the mornings. People came back; the shops

did good business and the dogs got their meals. Shingmo ate big meals. She was always hungry, and Thin often told her she would burst if she ate another morsel.

But she didn't.

She just grew.

Everybody said Shingmo was growing tall. Her legs grew long. Her tail grew longer. But her nose grew the longest—it was the first thing that greeted you, an eager snout, black and curious. Then you noticed her eyes: beautiful and big and brown, outlined carefully—as if by a skilled make-up artist—in black, and somehow always managing to look sad. No matter how much she ate, no matter how much she played, Shingmo always looked as if she was about to cry.

'Such a drama queen!' Krya scoffed, but even she was secretly pleased with the new puppy. She was a survivor, wasn't she?

'Shingmo, Thin!' Damu shouted when he came back, on the tenth day after the big rain. 'My house was flooded; we lost everything! These are new clothes. I had to go to the market and buy them. Don't tear them, okay?' he told them, picking Shingmo up and playing with her, patting Thin on her head and hugging her close.

'How did you manage to get fatter?' Damu poked Thin's tummy; he tickled all her chins. 'And you, Shingmo, you're such a big girl now!'

'Now can I go home?' Coconut asked.

'Okay, but if it rains again ...' Krya growled.

'I know, I'll come back ...' he said, beginning to walk away.

'Coconut, wait.' Krya went bounding up to him. 'You said someone died the day Shingmo arrived. Who was it?'

'Oh, that was my friend Sweetie—she lived near the park. I was very sad that day, but when it rained, I was glad she was gone. She wouldn't have come to the shops, you know ... the night she died, it was beautiful: there were many stars, and a half moon. The wind sang to her, and she went for one last walk and then, she, well ... the cleaning crew buried her near the pier. When I'm dead, that's where they'll take me ...' He coughed gently, and walked away slowly.

CHAPTER FIVE

My Name is Coconut

Are you sitting down comfortably? Okay, then let me tell you my story.

My name is Coconut and—what is it? You have a question? But I've barely begun ...

Oh well, if it's urgent, ask ...

Ah, you want to know why I'm called Coconut? That's what Didi called me.

She found me by the tender coconut stall near her college and took me to her hostel.

She loved me. She bathed me with soap and water and kisses. She fed me bread and milk and rice.

Unfortunately, the warden found me. It was my fault; don't blame Didi. I barked in the night when I heard the rats in the corridor.

The warden said I had to go.

If you can keep rats, why can't I keep a puppy? Didi argued.

The warden said, fine, keep your puppy on the pavement, get out now.

So Didi brought me here, in an autorickshaw, and she cried as if the world was going to end. She tied me to the coconut tree with a long rope, told me I had to be brave and then she went away.

I didn't feel very brave though. I was also very hungry, so I sat and chewed the rope, and when it grew dark, I went and hid behind the tree. The sea was scary—it kept saying 'shusha-shusha' all night; waves leapt up, some came hissing and running, and I thought they were hungry too, and they wanted to eat me for dinner ...

I don't know when I fell asleep, but when I opened my eyes, the sun was up, the sea was calm, and there was a roti on top of my head.

I thought Didi was back, but it was only a crow. It was sitting on top of the tree, holding another roti with its feet and tearing at it with its beak.

I ate mine hurriedly—what if the crow wanted it back?

But she didn't.

A little while later, she dropped me a piece of egg. I ate that too.

She became my friend. And I became her guard dog.

I protected her nest from cats and hawks, and in return, she brought me the finest scraps from the dustbin.

All this was fifteen years ago.

I helped her raise many broods, and I've watched over her great-grandchildren. Now I'm the oldest dog on the beach, and I want a nap, so please excuse me and go build your sandcastles. I'll speak to you later, okay?

🐾🐾🐾

You're still here?

Oh, you have a biscuit for me. How sweet! But I can't eat it ... my teeth are nearly gone, and what's there is very weak, so please give it to that crow over there? He's my friend's great-great-great-great grandson. I can only eat mush now—one uncle brings it for me in the night, when the world is asleep and the beach is finally empty, after the police have sent all the people home. Uncle comes on a cycle; he brings the food in a steel dabba, then he serves it on a newspaper. It's such tasty food, so easy to swallow. You must ask him the recipe and try it someday.

Maybe you'll—what? You have another question? Oh dear, you young people are full of questions.

You want to know what I eat during the day? Well, nothing much. I don't run around like before, so I don't get very hungry. My only job is to keep a careful eye on you all. Krya comes here anyway to discuss all the important matters.

Now if you'll keep quiet for a little while, I'll tell you about the dogs' beach.

No, it's not a separate beach; we sit and sleep on the same one, but it's different, you understand?

What do you mean you don't understand?

Hmm, try this then. Go down on your knees and hands—yes, on all fours. Now look at your house. Isn't everything taller? Isn't the ground closer? Can't you see what's on the floor better? That's how it is for us. Plus, our eyesight is so much sharper, really. And we can hear and smell very well. Do you know what someone's cooking four houses away? We do—we're clever like that.

But because we're small—and clever—we come in the way. Of people. And we're not very important. Or grand. Some dogs are grand, don't get me wrong. But they generally have lots of fur, and they're always very hot. They have to walk on leashes, poor things, and though they get good meals, I hear—come closer, I can't say this loudly—they get their tushies wiped. I mean, the whole idea is to smell powerful there. But those chaps? They smell like flowers. And baby powder. Disgusting!

So people chase us away. They call us dirty. They tell their children we'll bite. But we don't, not normally. You know why? Because we'll be punished. We'll lose our only home. And this is our home. You're our guests. Would you like some tea?

Thank god you said no; I have no money. Do you know what it is like to not have any money when there's so much you can buy and eat here?

There are stalls from every part of India. There is spicy food and sweet food and sour food and simple food. Do you like roast corn? You get the best ones here, freshly roasted over coals—the sparks go zing, zing, zing, and from afar it looks like a lot of bright insects flying for a second and then dying. There's chaat, so many kinds—with dahi, without dahi, with potato, without potato—but the one with potato and dahi is the best.

Then there's pizza—it smells of cheese, and people eat the middle and always leave the corners for us. I love chewing on those bits. Not now, of course—now I can't chew anything, but when I was young, I hunted for discarded corners and buried them under the sand, to eat later. Only sometimes the sea would come rushing in and take them away, and I would weep, thinking of the fish feasting on my hard work.

There are cool drinks of every colour kept in tall bottles! Purple, orange, yellow, green! And ice creams and water! Water! They give you water if you give them money. I've seen it with my own eyes—it's a bottle and it has a cap, and you bite it like this with your teeth and chew it, and water pours into your mouth. It feels wonderful, especially when it's very hot and you're very thirsty—that's when water's the only thing we want and that's the only thing we can't find ...

Of course, I know what you're going to say. Yes, we have this great big sea, but the water's very salty. We gag when we drink it. Only the fish like it. And turtles. Oh, and dolphins. Have you ever seen any? One time, during the big flood, a big, big dolphin washed up on this beach. It was quite dead, poor thing. The crows thought they had enough to eat for a month, but some important people came in a van and they took it away ...

If you have money, you can buy anything. But maybe even then you can't buy a house as big and beautiful as mine: this beach. Now, if you don't mind, I'm going to nap again—I'm old, I need a lot of sleep!—so come back another day …

What? Oh, you want one last story?

Okay, let me tell you about my friend. His name was Kaalu, and he was as black as I was white—they say I'm grey as an elephant now, although I don't know what an elephant is!—and he was three years older than me, and he loved fried food. Every day he ate bhujia and sev and pani-puri shells—he was such a charmer that people readily gave him half of what they were eating—but when he turned five, his sins came back to haunt his stomach. It rumbled and roared most days, and he starved himself and ate grass and the same people called him a great saint, for who else fasts like that for every festival of every religion, and they put a cushion for him outside the shrine—over there—and until he died, they took great care of him.

One day I too will be gone, but before that, I'll tell you everything I saw … but not now … now I'm sleepy …

The Disreputables

A gentle rain is a beautiful thing. And the rest of the monsoon was gentle. When the tide was low, the beach was long and sandy, and here and there tide pools formed, which the dogs used like great outdoor baths.

Shingmo loved the tide pools; she loved the sea. She was a fine swimmer, and she loved paddling over the waves to reach the rocks. Scrambling up, she would stand on them, a small dog on the tiny islands off the coast of Mumbai.

Shingmo loved to chase birds, and she went after all the crows and gulls. She sat and watched crabs, and played with shells. One time, when the beach was studded with blue jellyfish, she tried to smell them, and Thin yelled at her. She said they would sting so bad, Shingmo would be buried near Sweetie before sunset. And Shingmo sat and sulked under the coconut tree all day, all because Thin told her she could not walk on the beach blue with jellyfish ...

By the time she was four months old, Shingmo was already twice as fast as anybody else, both on land and in water. Thin watched her with maternal pride. She told Chocolate nobody could beat Shingmo in a race.

'Really?' someone said, and Thin turned her head. She froze. It was Thug.

He had wandered over from the Bad Side.

'Has she ever raced my boys?' he asked, and without waiting for an answer, he barked loudly.

Three dogs came running—they were large puppies, all of them, and their muscles were hard, their legs were strong, and they galloped like horses. They circled Thug and sat behind him tidily.

'Have you met them?' Thug asked in a silky voice. 'That's Laddu, this is Jalebi and this small, sharp one is Mirchi.'

Thin and Chocolate shivered when they heard him speak. They wished Krya, Big Head and Orange were there, but they were behind the shops, snoozing.

And Thug knew that; he was a cunning dog—his fur was grey like a stormy sky; his head was regal; his ears upright.

But Thug was also a real menace on the beach. He had attacked many dogs, and there was a rumour that one time, provoked needlessly, he nearly bit a human, and was taken away to a shelter for some days. When he came back, everybody said he was reformed. But not for long ...

It got worse when he started training pups. He picked freshly abandoned, small male puppies, taught them every dirty trick, and called them the 'Disreputables'. He encouraged them to steal food, harass house dogs and howl late in the night. Everybody was wary of his pack. Krya kept out of his way, and usually Thug didn't venture into her territory. Maybe his ego had been bruised that morning, or maybe he was bored. Clearly he was raring for a fight ...

He called out to Shingmo now. 'Come here, puppy, come, come.' But Shingmo knew something was wrong, and she hid behind Thin. 'Your foster mother says you can win a race against any dog; why don't you try these three?'

'Thug, she's only a puppy ...' Thin began.

'Then you mustn't brag; you must keep your mouth shut. Now that you've announced she's the fastest, prove it! Boys, come on. You pick which direction you want to run!'

'We'll go towards the hotel,' Laddu said.

That was the Good Side.

Chocolate and Thin hoped Coconut would be around—he could stop the dogs if they tried to attack Shingmo.

'Sure,' Thug said, 'but stay close to the water; there's an old dog by the trees and he's a pain—such a goody-goody ...'

Thin's face fell when she heard Thug.

She decided she would run behind the dogs, just in case, but—as if he had read her thoughts—Thug announced, 'And you, me and Chocolate will stay right here!'

The pups got ready for their race.

Shingmo crouched on the ground, every muscle alert and eager, ready to take off. Thug's puppies stood side by side, excited and hyper, and when Thug said 'go', they took off, all four, Shingmo easily the fastest, a small reddish-brown dog, running as if her life depended on it ...

In a couple of minutes, it appeared as if her life indeed depended on it. For Thug's pups were annoyed. They were angry. They were losing. So they decided to cheat. They turned on Shingmo, snarling at her and barking.

Shingmo was upset. This is not fair, she thought, and looked for help. There was nobody nearby. She decided to run into the water—that's what Thin had told her to do. Except, she was outnumbered and feared she would lose the fight. Laddu, Jalebi and Mirchi came closer, their jaws snapping, and their hackles standing up in clumps. Shingmo's stood up in fright. But just when Mirchi caught her tail, a loud voice called out, 'Stop it! Stop Hounding her!' and a plump lady puffed and panted towards the sea. Before she could reach there, her dog did—a white and black bullet that came charging at Mirchi and snapped at his face. Next, the dog bared all her

teeth—and they were big and sharp and white—at Laddu and Jalebi.

'Go back, you bullies,' the dog told Thug's pups. 'You're rotten, you're rogues, you're savages!'

And the three, not used to being told off, not knowing what to do—Thug was still far away—backed down. They tucked their tails between their legs and slunk away quietly.

Shingmo stood shivering in the water. The dog went back to the lady, who patted her black and white head lovingly. She told her over and over, 'What a good girl Puchu is!' and the dog danced around her legs. 'Come now, little one,' Puchu's human called

Shingmo, and she went to her slowly. The lady picked up the trembling dog, folded her in her arms and stroked her soft head.

Then she kissed each ear and tickled her stomach, and when the pup was calm, she walked back with her.

'You live there, don't you, with Krya's gang? We've seen you from afar. We walk on that side. You're really cute; we'll come and see you every day from now on, okay?'

By then Thin had reached them. She came up to greet the newcomers.

Puchu froze when she came closer.

The two females stood facing each other, shoulder to shoulder, their faces stiff, whiskers alert, ears erect, and when they were sure the other wasn't the least bit threatening, gently sniffed each other's backside.

'Now you come here and sniff her bottom,' Thin instructed Shingmo. 'That's how dogs say hullo.'

Shingmo came near Puchu's rear and gasped. 'Oh no! Thin, Puchu's tail is missing!' she cried. 'There's only a bit here—come, come, let's look for the rest of it! It must have fallen near the water!'

Puchu was amused. 'Nobody in my family has one,' she explained, wriggling her tiny tail for effect.

'Did all of you lose it?' Shingmo asked, wide-eyed with worry and disbelief. 'How careless!'

'No,' Puchu said patiently, 'we were all born without much a tail.'

Shingmo was, by then, very puzzled. She cocked her head to one side and asked softly, 'Puchu, are you sure you're a dog?'

Puchu growled softly. 'Pup, you're rude, you know that?' she said, and was about to deliver a lecture, but just then her mother called her and told her it was time they went home. So Puchu just walked away in a huff, while Shingmo watched, fascinated, as Puchu's bum moved from side to side, and her little stump of a tail wobbled behind her.

CHAPTER SEVEN

Feeling Friendless

The monsoon was nearly over. It was September, and the sun was back. It blazed high in the sky in the afternoons; the sand was hot to the touch, the sky blue and cloudless. Mornings and evenings were pleasant, and the beach was beautiful but crowded. Business was brisk by the shops, and smaller businesses came up on the dogs' territory too—bottles of colourful drinks, freshly assembled chaat, coconut water, hair clips, balloons, beads ... all were sold and bought with enthusiasm.

Children came with their families. They were mostly told never to go near the dogs. But they were rarely told never to throw sand on a dog. Many, therefore, thought it was their duty to chuck some on a sleeping stray dog. But the animals were patient. Shingmo was the most patient of all.

Shingmo loved people. When she saw a friendly face, she squealed, flopped on the ground, presented her belly for a rub and cried when she wasn't petted. She ran behind the beach regulars. Many said 'shoo', but one or two said 'cute puppy', and she came back and told Thin she was the cutest puppy and that everybody loved her.

Shingmo also loved to play. Any piece of rubbish became a toy. She picked up the plastic or paper humans left behind, carrying it carefully in her mouth, and invited Thin to play. But Thin never wanted to. She would lick Shingmo, and tell her she was busy (sleeping) and to come back later. So Shingmo would go and ask Chocolate, but she always said she was busy (sleeping) too. Sometimes Chocolate and Thin went off on their important business. Once Shingmo followed them, only to find they went and slept near the shrine. It was the perfect spot for a snooze—it was sunny, but the coconut trees also threw some shade, and nobody disturbed them. Shingmo wished she had energetic friends. Everybody in her gang was either lazy or too grand to play with her.

That's why she was delighted when Puchu began hanging out with them.

Puchu came to meet the gang every morning.

Mother would bring her to the beach, take off Puchu's leash, look at her phone for a while, then she'd sigh and sit on the sand and dream. The dogs would gather, they'd gallop, and they would gossip.

'How come you never run with me?' Shingmo asked Krya.

'Because you're a baby,' she snapped.

'Oh, all right,' Shingmo said good-naturedly, and ran in front. She remained fast; the others were no match, but Puchu nearly caught up with her a few times.

When the tide was low, they had the most fun. They clambered up the rocks, leapt from one to the other, turned over the big orange conches, leapt back when crabs peered out, chased fishermen's boats and harassed timid house dogs.

Most weren't allowed to play with them. 'Don't go near them!' their humans yelled. 'Strays are dirty; they have worms!'

Shingmo was puzzled whenever she heard them.

'But we don't have worms, do we?' she asked Thin.

'Damu brings us medicines to kill them,' Thin explained. 'But they're not very tasty.'

'Please! You don't eat medicines because they're tasty. I have vitamins every morning!' Puchu explained solemnly.

'Oh! Are you very sick?' Shingmo asked, worried. 'Or,' she whispered, mischievously, 'is it to make your tail grow?'

'You're irritating me,' Puchu growled. 'Leave my tail alone, will you?' And with that she stalked off.

Shingmo felt dreadful. Would she ever come back to play with her?

For a few days, Puchu did not.

She walked with the house dogs and played with them in the water. They lounged on the sand, dug holes and stomped on the previous day's sand castles. And all the while, beach walkers fussed over them.

'How handsome!' they said, patting Puchu's friend, a beautiful Husky called Xyro.

'How cute!' they said, hugging a tiny Chihuahua called Potato.

People took selfies with the Husky; they made videos of the Labradors; they praised the Beagles for finding food.

And they ignored the strays.

The strays also ignored Shingmo.

'You're annoying,' they said.

Krya nipped her when she tried to go close. Thin put up with her, but she mostly slept, because it was hot. Chocolate growled; Big Head and Orange barked.

Shingmo told Damu all about it.

He heard a series of squeals. 'You sound like a buffalo!' He laughed, and hugged her.

'Nobody loves me, and I love everybody; this is not fair!' Shingmo said over and over, and Damu said, 'I love you, puppy' as if he understood, and he cuddled her.

'Come, let's go for a walk,' he said, and took her over to see Baby Diane and Fat Brother. 'Maybe you need to spend more time with puppies.'

But Baby Diane and Fat Brother were very nearly dogs. And they were very hungry dogs. They had one aim in life—to find food. And they were bothered they couldn't find it easily.

'Hey, you,' they asked Shingmo, 'are you a good hunter?'

'Why, yes!' Shingmo said. 'I can run very fast. I nearly caught a pigeon once, and one time there was a crow that—'

'Uff, no!' the twins cried. 'Food. Can you find food? Nice human food? Roti, bun, biscuit ... that sort of thing!'

'Ah, you mean treats from the dustbins?' Shingmo asked.

'Never!' said Baby Diane.

'Never,' said Fat Brother. 'We only eat from the sand. We have standards, you know ...'

'You should ask the Beagles,' Shingmo told them. 'They seem to be experts!'

'Good idea,' the twins said. 'But what are Beagles?'

'Those house dogs that always look down, keep their tails up and eat as they walk ...'

'Ah, those! We know them—Bob and Bilbo. Their humans are always shouting at them. We'll ask them, thanks.' And they went away together, to tell Coconut their plan. They found Coconut sleeping in the shade, snoring loudly, and they felt a snooze coming. So they curled up 'just for five minutes' and woke up at five in the evening ...

Meanwhile, Shingmo spent the afternoon sighing—she wanted a friend. She decided to find one. She went around looking for a kindly face. Most people were napping. She went near the shops, but Thug was sitting there, and the Disreputables were nearby, so she scooted to the other side. She caught a scent in the air ... it smelt familiar. She sniffed the sand again. Yes, it was ... Puchu ... and over there, her mother. Maybe she could find them and tell Puchu she wouldn't talk about her tail again. She followed the scent with her head down, nose to the ground. It took her under a gate, over a lawn, by some cars, past two bikes, near a big grey door ... and then it was gone.

Shingmo was puzzled. How did they vanish? Did the door eat them? She sniffed at the bottom carefully, she sniffed the side, and she almost lost her nose, because just then the door opened and out came ... Puchu's mother!

'Shingmo!' she said, and Shingmo ran to her, her whole body trembling with excitement. 'What are you doing here? Did you run away from the beach? Did you come to see Puchu? Come with me. Let's go find her ...' And she carried Shingmo in the lift.

Shingmo's stomach felt odd when the lift moved. She barked. Mother soothed her.

She opened the door again, and this time she rang a bell, and suddenly the corridor was filled with a terrible barking.

'Puchu, it's your friend Shingmo!' Mother said when the door opened. 'Be nice!'

But Puchu was not planning to be nice. She was not happy to see Shingmo, and she made that very clear. She barked and barked at the puppy. She growled loudly, she showed her teeth and all her hackles stood up.

'Take her away,' Puchu said. 'This is my house!'

When Mother tried to come in, Puchu jumped on her and tried to nip Shingmo.

The puppy was frightened. She had never seen Puchu so angry or aggressive. She clung onto Mother, she tried to climb on her shoulder, she wriggled, she jumped down, and she blindly ran down the stairs, as if a monster was chasing her, until somehow she reached the ground floor. She ran faster then, until she saw the parked bikes and cars and lawn and, finally, the gate to the beach.

She was home. She was friendless. She cried herself to sleep ...

CHAPTER EIGHT

A Feast and Some Festivals

Shingmo thought she was dreaming. One minute she had been fast asleep, her belly warmed by the sun, her paws stretched in different directions, tongue lolling, eyes rolling, dreaming of friends and playtime, and the next, a dog was licking her ears gently. And it wasn't just any dog—it was Puchu. Shingmo was happy, of course, but she was also scared. Was she licking her ears to see how she tasted? Would she eat her up next? Startled, she backed away swiftly and bumped into something large ... It was Puchu's mother, smiling at her. She had biscuits in her hand, some of which she offered Shingmo.

The puppy ate them gratefully. She chomped them with her mouth open, spraying crumbs everywhere, drooling over Mother's hand, her black whiskers turning a biscuity brown.

'Messy baby!' Mother laughed and wiped her mouth and face with her dupatta.

Shingmo climbed on Mother's lap; she licked her nose.

'Gosh, you're smelly.' Mother laughed some more, pushing her away. 'I wish I could take you home and bathe you properly!'

Puchu glared at Mother, then she looked away.

After Shingmo had run away, Mother had scolded Puchu. She had told her she was a terrible dog, an embarrassment—whatever that was—and that they were ashamed of her. That cut badly. Puchu wanted them to be proud of her. So she decided she'd apologise to that annoying puppy. But now Mother was talking of bringing her home again. Didn't she know how insecure she was about new creatures?

'Come here, Puchu. You have a biscuit too,' Mother called.

Puchu went up to her and took one delicately and ate it thoughtfully. Not a crumb fell from her mouth. Mother praised Puchu for 'good eating'. Shingmo was full of admiration.

'What lovely manners you have, Puchu,' she said.

That pleased Puchu; she felt very flattered.

'All right,' she said gruffly, 'all right. We can be friends again. Just don't be so clingy, and get off my mother's lap, will you?'

Shingmo obeyed her, but she was puzzled: why wouldn't she share her mother? After all, Puchu played with her foster mother, Thin. And Shingmo didn't mind, did she?

But she decided not to say anything. She was happy her friend was back.

She asked her shyly, 'Can we go for a walk?' When Puchu said okay, Shingmo ran ahead quickly until she was near the water. The sun painted the far sea orange, the waves rushed up to meet the sand, then back to meet the rocks, and the dogs played 'catch-me-if-you-can'. And then, when they were fully tired, they lay down on their sides and watched the sky turn dark and broody. They went back to Mother reluctantly, and hung their heads when she scolded them for being dirty. Dirty, sandy dogs they were, but very happy dogs, with lolling tongues ...

Very soon, their beach got busy again. And this time, it was with the big festivals that came one after the other. Ganesh Chaturthi. Dussehra. Diwali. People came to the beach to celebrate all of them;

they brought great big idols of Ganpati Bappa and Ma Durga, took them deep into the sea on boats and submerged them. Large crowds gathered in the evenings. They brought with them food and flowers—and left a lot of these behind. Watch towers went up, where the police stood and scanned the crowd for troublemakers. Barricades were put up. Safety measures were announced through loudspeakers: parents were asked to take care of their children, and everybody was asked to take care of their belongings.

Nobody had the time to take care of the dogs. Most days they slept on top of the watchtower, the whole gang climbing up after people had gone home. Sometimes a few drunk men climbed up after them, and kicked a dog or three down to make room for themselves. Once Shingmo was thrown down from the top. She landed on loose sand, unhurt.

What truly frightened the dogs was loud noises. And Shingmo was especially scared of firecrackers. She could manage everything else, even the great thirst on hot days—for their water bowl was routinely misused by the visiting public, to wash their slippers—and learnt to lick the blooming dampness around drain pipes. But she was terrified of the boom-dhoom and the rockets and the bursts of bright colours in the sky. One day, when the noise was especially bad, she ran helter-skelter; she ran towards the sea, towards the trees, but the sounds and lights followed her everywhere. She ran, without realising it, towards Thug and the Disreputables. They surrounded and taunted her. She whimpered and howled and shivered, but this time Krya came running. She swiped at Thug, she snapped at Laddu, Mirchi and Jalebi, and she escorted the sorry-looking puppy back to her beach.

'Shingmo, I know you're scared,' Krya told her kindly and affectionately, 'but this is how it is. You've got to get used to it.'

But Shingmo simply couldn't. That night, she developed a fever. The next day, she was very ill. She lay there on the sand, unable to lift her head, unable to eat a morsel. Thin was worried. She waited till Damu came, then barked to get his attention, and he followed at once.

Except, Damu said he wouldn't be able to help. 'I think it's the crackers; she's just too scared. What if she dies of fright?'

Puchu's mother saw him stroking Shingmo. She had just come to the beach for a walk.

'Oh, what happened to the puppy?' she asked.

'She's not even able to stand; she's in a state of shock,' Damu said, picking up Shingmo and placing her on his shoulders. But the puppy slid down, falling like a rag doll on the sand.

Mother gave Puchu's leash to Damu.

'Hold her,' she said, and picked up Shingmo in her arms like a baby.

'I'm going to rush her to the vet. My husband will come to pick up Puchu. Please will you mind her till then?'

Mother ran to the main road, the pup panting in her arms. She hailed an autorickshaw and went straight to the vet.

'Emergency!' she cried.

The vet asked her to place Shingmo on a stainless steel table. 'Her blood pressure's very high,' the vet said. 'She might have had a seizure because of that.'

And so they began her treatment.

Because she was very young—and her heart and body were otherwise healthy—Shingmo responded well. She was out of danger in a few hours. All through, Mother stayed by her side. And Father joined them after dropping Puchu home.

'We can't put her back on the beach. Should we foster her for a few days?' Mother asked.

'We don't have a choice. She won't survive otherwise,' Father replied.

'But what about Puchu? She will not be pleased!' Mother said, worried.

'She'll have to lump it!' Father said, and he looked determined to make her accept the puppy.

In Pursuit of Pink Ears

The first two days Shingmo was home—and she was now a lovely, sleek seven-month-old puppy—Puchu put up with her. She understood she was sick. She watched her sleep. And when she woke up, she came and fetched Mother.

'She's reformed,' Girl said. Girl was Puchu's human sister, and she had bunked college to look after Shingmo.

'I don't know,' Mother said, confused. 'Do you think this will last? Anyway, today's the last vet visit; let's get her vaccinations going and her ears cleaned. They smell poooeeeey!'

'Are we taking Puchu too?' Father asked.

'Why not!' Girl said, and got leashes and collars for both dogs.

So the whole family went to the vet.

First, Puchu's ears were cleaned. And then Mother placed Shingmo on the steel table. The vet's assistant rolled a wad of damp cotton, and inside the ear it went. Shingmo pulled a face, clenched her teeth, bent her head and made an odd noise. The cotton came out pungent and black.

The assistant glared at Shingmo, glared at Mother, rolled another long piece of cotton between his fingers, and this time, when he pulled it out, it was brown.

'Why is she so filthy?' the assistant asked, cleaning the ear one last time, and this time, the cotton came out cream coloured, and the ears were pretty and pink. 'Better,' he said, and patted the

puppy's head. Shingmo looked at him with liquid eyes, her eyebrows gathering as if she was about to cry. The assistant felt so guilty, he told her he was very sorry, and left the room with his head hanging. Mother and Father laughed.

'She's a crafty one, isn't she?' they said.

'Go easy on the praise; someone's getting jealous,' Girl said, and pointed to Puchu, who had puffed out her lips in anger.

'Woof, woof,' she warned, and everybody laughed. Puchu decided this was getting out of hand. She had to teach them a lesson ...

But first, the family learnt a lesson on their own.

Shingmo had been prescribed two syrups. The vet had helpfully told them that they could use a syringe—without a needle—to squirt the liquid into her mouth. So Mother carefully measured 5 ml, Father held Shingmo's head, and put the syringe close to her face ... drenching all of them with its contents. Shingmo had firmly shut her mouth.

She fought to free herself from Father's hand, snapped at the syringe, took it in her mouth and ran a victory lap around the table. As Shingmo ran, Girl laughed hysterically, while Puchu chased Shingmo to grab the syringe from her.

'I thought she was a small, sweet puppy,' Mother said, wiping syrup from her face.

'Sweet? She's savage; her teeth are like needles!' Father said, rubbing his wounded hands.

'What do we do?' they asked, watching the dogs wrestle on the floor, the syringe a mangled piece of plastic, their fur pink and sticky with syrup.

'How I wish she'd learn to be nice and civilised like Puchu!' Mother sighed.

In five minutes, she ate her words.

Puchu had had enough. Shingmo was getting better, but she wasn't going away, plus everybody was fussing over her—Mother did not even find the time anymore to tell her 'what a good girl Puchu is', which was their special song. The new pup slept on her bed, she ate from her bowl, and ohhh, now she was going to take her favourite stuffed toy: the platypus.

'Shingmo!' Puchu barked loudly in her face.

The puppy got frightened, and she dropped the platypus.

Puchu circled Shingmo slowly, her fur standing on end, growling menacingly, and suddenly, she attacked the puppy viciously.

Mother, Father and Girl watched, horrified, as Puchu and Shingmo fought bitterly, rolling on the ground, running around the room, leaping on the table, the side table, the sofa, and flipping cushions, indoor plants, piles of books ...

GRRR!

The neighbours came to ask if someone was murdering a dog; the crows in the nearby trees cawed loudly in accompaniment; Mother wept, Father groaned, and even Girl couldn't laugh anymore.

'Right,' she said, 'these two are going to separate rooms. Puchu, you come here with me; you're a disgrace.' She dragged the crotchety dog to her bedroom.

Mother and Father checked Shingmo. She wasn't badly hurt, just a scratch here and there. This was going to be hard, they thought, and it certainly was, the first few days. But slowly, very slowly, Puchu got used to Shingmo, and the puppy learnt to respect and obey the older dog.

'But she's still quite annoying; how did you put up with her?' Puchu asked Thin one evening, when Shingmo was lovingly chewing her foster mother's ear.

'I miss her, Puchu,' Thin said, and then she yelped. Shingmo had bitten off her whiskers.

'You stupid dog,' Thin roared. 'Come back here,' she howled, but Shingmo ran far away, a healthy, confident puppy, with strong muscles and a shiny coat.

'Didn't I say she'll be a beauty?' Damu told Gautam, watching Shingmo from a distance and sighing happily. 'Now please will you give me a cup of tea? I'm broke today.' He grinned.

'I'm so surprised,' Gautam said mischievously. The two men sipped tea companionably, Thin and Puchu sat together, and Shingmo chased a white bird flying low over the grey sea. In the distance, the sun set, orange and round. Shingmo came back and sat next to the older dogs and begged: 'Puchu, please tell me your story again?'

CHAPTER TEN

My Name is Puchu

Listen carefully, Shingmo. I'm going to tell you my story one last time.

No, not even one more time after this; don't make puppy eyes at me. They won't work, sorry—oh, don't cry! Why do you always look so sad?

Fine, maybe just another time, but don't ask me tomorrow, okay?

Okay, let me begin. My name is Puchu and—

What?

Okay, I will begin in the gutter.

I was born in a stinky gutter, near a fancy shopping mall in Mumbai. My mother was white-faced and beautiful, but I was a white and black fur ball—my brother and sister were also spotty and plump, like me. All of us had lavish whiskers, but none of us had much of a tail.

When I was three weeks old, my mum started teaching us worldly stuff. She told us about rowdy dogs and foul bandicoots, and told us to keep away from them. Whenever she leapt out for a meal, she warned us to stay quiet and safe. She usually came back licking her lips—a kindly lady, she explained, brought her rice and chicken—and then snoozed next to us.

Mum told us about the animals outside the gutter.

'Cats are evil, especially the ones with yellow eyes. Crows are very clever; pigeons are very stupid,' she explained. 'And there are cockroaches.' Mum pointed to the creatures on the walls of the gutter, with brown wings and antennae. 'Squish them, but don't eat them. It disgusts humans.'

'How do you know, mummy?' I had asked her, rubbing my face on mum's neck.

'I was a house dog once,' mum replied, a faraway look in her eye.

When I asked her what had happened, she just said, 'Sleep, my baby, shhh, sleep,' and licked my face and tummy till I slept.

In a few weeks, winter came to the gutter. The water turned cold. All of us pups shivered, and our soggy fur shook. Mum looked worried. She grew thinner, we grew bigger; she ate less, we wanted more. So when the kindly lady took us away, promising to find us nice homes, mum was … not happy to see us go, but hopeful; she was definitely hopeful.

But I was terrified, Shingmo—I had never been outside the gutter. It was very bright, very loud. And there was nothing soft and warm to hug. But a family adopted me. They were kind initially—they scrubbed me clean and wiped my ears. They gave me warm milk in a bowl. Of course, I missed my mum, my family. But I was happy with my new one.

Except … in a few weeks, there was a new baby in the house.

Suddenly everything changed.

The little human cried all the time. It was loud and smelly, but somehow people liked it. Do you know, it couldn't even walk? They had to carry it everywhere!

But once the baby arrived, they lost interest in me.

The only thing they told me was 'shoo'; they forgot to give me my meals. I grew thinner and sadder, and they told me if nobody wanted to keep me (they had asked their friends), they were going to leave me again, by the gutter near the mall.

That's when Mother found me.

She had heard through some friends that I was up for adoption. She took me home, and for the first few days, I trembled and refused to let them hug me. What if they, too, got bored with me in a few days and wanted to send me back? What if another small

creature came—like you!—and they liked it better than me? I was always worried. But soon I began to trust them. And after that we all lived happily, until …

Now do you understand why I was so upset with you? I thought I'd be sent away again, Shingmo.

What? Oh, you want me to tell you about the toilet training?

Well, Mother taught me that the house was where we ate and slept, and everything else had to happen downstairs. She usually walked around with newspapers and poop bags, but in the beginning I thought it was a game. We'd go downstairs, stand under the coconut tree, Mother would say 'sssss, sssss' and people would smile at her and smile at me, and we'd go back home again. Then I'd pee in the kitchen, and Mother would scold me. I never really understood what she wanted me to do, you know. In my old gutter, there was such a bouquet of rich aromas. I could pee anywhere; my mum never barked at me. But Girl was very patient. She trained me, and Mother and Father gave her a treat. And as a special treat, Girl let me sleep on the mat outside her bathroom. Life smelt so much better!

Becoming a house dog wasn't easy, you know, Shingmo. First you need to learn so many languages. Do you know each of them speaks a different one? I know four. What? You know more languages than me? Oh, right. You have lived with more people ... but surely you can't speak five!

Wait that's right—you do understand English, Tamil, Hindi, Marathi, Gujarati. Hmm, you're clever, Shingmo.

But I know more tricks than you, Shingmo. When I was a puppy, a trainer came home and taught me stuff. She was fun—she smelt like a pack of dogs, and she spoke Dog, you know. Thin, have you ever been trained? Maybe small things, like come, sit, shake hands? I was taught so many 'tricks'. Many of them are silly, but what to do, one has to humour humans. They get very excited about little things—like when I catch a biscuit. I mean,

how hard is it, really? You can see it coming close to your mouth; all you have to do is open your mouth on time. Then they give you another biscuit because you've caught the first one. My family is quite simple, really.

But I have also had to work on training them.

In the beginning, they just didn't understand me.

Mother, especially, was always anxious. Whenever she felt cold, she made me wear a sweater. Whenever she felt hot, I sat in the AC room—do you know about ACs, Thin? Stop jumping, Shingmo—I know you've seen one. Thin hasn't. Shouldn't we explain it to her?

Thin, it's a box from which cool air comes. It soon makes the whole room cold and then we fall asleep under a quilt and wake up hours later for a warm meal ...

Oh Thin, I'm sorry ... I didn't mean to make you feel bad. So thoughtless of me. Shingmo, look, it's all your fault.

What do you mean why? You're small, you're easy to blame, besides what else are little sisters for?

The Great Hunt

Winter came very soon. And it brought with it a great playfulness. The dogs were in fine spirits, especially when their stomachs were half full. But that wasn't always easy. Fewer people came to the beach—it was a little too chilly to sit by the sea late into the evening—and there were few food stalls. Still, the dogs managed—they scrounged, they survived. They had no choice!

Krya had a special walk in the colder months. She crisscrossed her front legs and leapt high with every step. It looked as if she were dancing. Maybe she wanted to ...

She also took great pleasure in chasing pigeons. People left a lot of grain for them on the sand. The birds gathered there, forming a noisy grey carpet, and got to work quickly, polishing off the food. Krya would wait until they were nicely settled. Then she'd come running from a distance and cut right through the pigeons. Startled, the birds would fly in every direction, a thousand grey wings beating, and through that cloud of feathers, she would emerge, golden and beautiful, the Don of the beach.

Thin didn't care for such games. She was a simple dog, and her wants were small: some food, water, a place to sleep, and occasionally a friend to roam around with. After Shingmo went to Puchu's house, she sat with Chocolate or Coconut in the evenings. When her friends came for a walk with Mother, she ran with them and played with them, and petted her foster daughter. Usually she sat on Mother's feet, and begged her not to go back home. Mother wept. 'Oh baby,' she said, over and over, pressing her forehead to Thin's, 'you're such a loyal dog!'

Shingmo was also a loyal dog. She pulled at her leash every day to go and meet Damu. 'You're growing big!' he would tell her, and scratch her ears.

Then she would drag Mother towards the sea. That's where she found the travelling plastic dabba. She called Puchu and Thin, and together they chased the dabba, which rolled about in the wind and made a rattling noise. It collected sand in its grooves and water in its mouth and waited for the dogs to catch it.

Puchu, Shingmo and Thin had a great time playing football and dog-ball with it. When a big wind came and took the dabba into the sea, they swam after it, but then they found half a coconut shell ...

On dark wintry mornings, fogs rolled in and quietly ate the tops of buildings. On clear days after the full moon, the beach was wide and wet and turned into a gigantic mirror, and the dogs and their reflections marched to the sound of the sea. Nights were beautiful, but they were also brutally cold. The homeless people who lived there piled coal and paper and wood and lit small, orange fires. They sat around them, rubbing their hands, pulling their shawls closer. Once they slept, the dogs gathered around the embers—they gave off a little warmth—scratched the sand a few times, rolled themselves into tight balls and shut their eyes.

One morning, Puchu and Shingmo were still sleeping with their eyes tightly shut when Mother and Father woke them up. They shook them by the shoulders and told them they must get ready.

'We're going on an adventure!' they said.

'What's an adventure, Puchu?' Shingmo asked sleepily.

'I think it's a kind of cake. With chicken. And biscuits,' Puchu replied dreamily.

'But why are they making us wear coats to eat a cake?' Shingmo asked, puzzled, when Girl slipped on their jackets.

'Get into the car!' Father said, and off they went.
After many hours—of barking at traffic signals and cars and cows—they reached a forest. The humans called it a resort. They got down from the

car and told the dogs to behave. They did—until Shingmo saw a squirrel. Then she ran after the squirrel, Puchu ran after Shingmo, and Mother and Father and Girl ran after the dogs.

'Bad puppy! Very bad puppy!' Girl scolded Shingmo after she caught her.

'What if we lost you, Shingmo?' Mother asked, hugging her. 'You don't know how to come back, do you?'

'This is turning out to be a bigger adventure than we bargained for!' Father said, wiping his sweaty forehead.

'Adventure was never a chicken cake with biscuits, Puchu,' Shingmo said sadly.

'No, Shingmo, but every day with you feels like one.' Puchu sighed.

Baby Diane and Fat Brother were also going on an adventure: Bob and Bilbo were taking them on a Great Hunt. It began when the twins asked the Beagles for help.

'Please, sir, could you teach us how to become fine hunters like you?'

The Beagles looked up when they heard 'sir'. Nobody had called them sir. They felt grand.

'We're feeling a bit sore here,' the twins told them, pressing their stomachs. 'We didn't find much to eat.'

The Beagles felt sorry. They, too, always felt sore in the middle and constantly craved food.

'Sure,' they said, 'we'll teach you. But not today.'

The twins' faces fell.

'Why not?' they chorused.

'Because we ate everything,' Bilbo said, smacking his lips.

'Meet us outside the hotel tomorrow morning at 7.15,' Bob said.

'Yes, we'll bring our mum and dad with us,' Bilbo said.

Baby Diane and Fat Brother were up at 6.15 the next morning.

They bounded up to the hotel. They sat on the steps and waited.

Bilbo and Bob trotted up soon.

'We need to lose our parents,' they said. 'We'll take them that side, near their friends. Then they'll sit around and chat, and we'll go on the hunt, okay?'

The twins nodded enthusiastically.

The Beagles were back in five minutes.

'Right.' Bilbo said. 'Here's the first thing you need to do—look at the sand carefully; wherever it is uneven, there's probably food beneath. Watch where the crows are; they'll lead you to food. Look around people; they always drop stuff. And lastly, trust your nose; it is one of the finest in the animal kingdom!'

'Wow, you're clever!' the twins said admiringly.

'Oh, it's nothing,' Bilbo said. 'I just read a lot of books.'

'I love books too!' Fat Brother said, closing his eyes and drooling a little bit. 'They're so chewy, so tasty ...'

'Look,' Bob said, 'do you want to hunt or not? It's getting late!'

'We're coming!' the twins said, and they went around, nose to the ground, following every instruction, and they found pooris and pav buns and pieces of bone. They ate all of it quickly, and thanked the Beagles profusely.

'Our pleasure,' Bilbo and Bob said. 'There's enough poori in the world for everyone.'

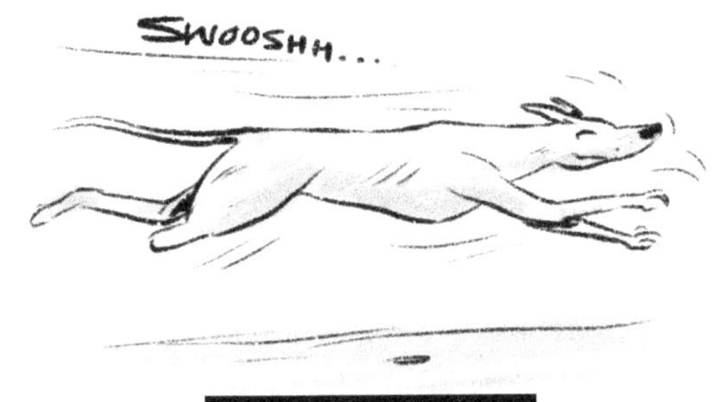

CHAPTER TWELVE

'Don't Give Up, Brown Girl!'

When Shingmo was ten months old, something really big happened: she became the second fastest runner on the beach. Why did she lose the first place? Well, here's how it came about.

One day, the twins were cross, and they were muttering and complaining to Coconut. 'We feel left out,' Baby Diane said.

'Very left out,' Fat Brother chorused.

'Why aren't you going on hunts with Bob and Bilbo?' Coconut asked, peering into the sea. 'And who are those new dogs?'

'That's why we're cross,' the twins cried. 'Those dogs are Bob and Bilbo's new family members, and now they can't hunt with us—they have to mind those two pups!'

'Doesn't look like minding to me,' Coconut said. 'They're lying on the sand, looking in the opposite direction! Besides, haven't you learnt how to hunt now? Go and find your pooris, shoo!'

But the twins waddled over to the Beagles instead.

'We miss you!' they said. 'Come back!'

'How I wish,' Bilbo said. 'I have a new sister; Bob has a new brother. And we're just sick of this child minding!'

'Can't you tell your parents?' the twins asked, puzzled.

'Not so easy,' Bob said, in his saddest voice. 'They're crazy about my brother. He's adopted, you know. I'll have to break it to him someday. Meanwhile, I'm supposed to guide him, and teach him, and if I don't share things with him, my food, my bed, my toys and my snacks are given to him—and all I get are smacks!'

'And my parents dote on my sister. They adopted her from some shelter too,' Bilbo said. 'Can you imagine our fate?' he sighed, and it was a deep long sigh, and the twins felt sorry for him.

'Is there anything we can do to help?' they asked sweetly, sincerely.

'Can you find us something to eat? A light snack would do nicely, thank you.' Bob licked his lips.

'Yes, a few theplas, one or two pav buns, a few potato chips ... let's see how much you've learnt!' Bilbo said.

And the twins went at once, saying 'yes, sir, of course, sir', while the Beagles sat back and waited.

Baby Diane and Fat Brother were back in five minutes. Each had a biscuit in their mouth. They had found theplas, they confessed, but they smelt of ghee and were begging to be eaten, so they had to oblige.

'But here's a biscuit nobody wanted, not even the crows, but since you eat everything ...' The twins shrugged, and since Bob and Bilbo indeed ate everything, they chomped the biscuits down.

'Right—now we have to go back home,' the Beagles said, and barked to get their siblings' attention.

'Not now,' two dogs barked back from the sea. They were white blurs, racing each other by the waves. One was fast, the other faster, and they sped, from one side to the other, and back again. As he watched, Fat Brother told Baby Diane he was getting dizzy.

'I need to lie down; I'm exhausted just looking at them,' Baby Diane said. Fat Brother said he fully agreed, and the two of them shuffled off to nap under the trees.

After ten minutes of stern barking, the siblings came out of the water. The Beagles were relieved, their parents were relieved, but the siblings ran back home before all of them.

'You should have seen them, Shingmo!' the twins told her the next morning. 'We thought those dogs had wings!'

They embroidered the truth here and there: the dogs' wings were wider than an eagle's; they flew over the water; and when they landed, fish jumped out onto the sand, gasping.

Shingmo felt a twinge of jealousy.

Who, she thought, could be faster than her?

'Hmm,' she said, 'I don't trust you two. Maybe you had too much to eat, and you were dreaming up stuff…'

'Oh, we were practically starving,' the twins said, sucking in their stomachs. 'Which reminds us, maybe we should hunt a little?'

As soon as the twins trotted off, tenderly, hopefully, sniffing the sand, Shingmo ran to Puchu.

'Did you hear?' she asked, hot and bothered by what she had just heard.

'Dogs don't have wings, Shingmo. They're lying,' Puchu said wisely.

Just then, as if to prove her wrong, two dogs went running by the sea. They shot through the water, their legs barely hitting the ground, their bodies trim and narrow and leaping, leaping …

'Wow,' Puchu said, 'just look at them!'

'Puchu, don't be a traitor!' Shingmo cried. 'I'm the fastest on this beach, remember?'

'But it's okay, Shingmo,' Puchu consoled her. 'There can be others better than you!'

But Shingmo howled, and she threw a small

tantrum: the Beagles looked up from their snooze—they were 'minding' their siblings from the sand—and the twins looked up from their scrounging; even Coconut woke up from his sleep.

'Behave yourself, Shingmo; you're making a scene,' Puchu said, embarrassed. 'Mother will drag us back home.'

'Oh, she's busy chatting with the Beagles' fathers. I'm going to challenge those new dogs to a race—that's what I will do.' And so, determined, she ran towards the sea.

'Oi, you two!' she barked to get their attention.

The two dogs slowed down, turning to look at her, then they came running, and Shingmo was shocked ... one dog had only three legs; the other dog had a broken paw.

'Oh,' she said awkwardly, 'I'm sorry, I didn't know ...'

'That's okay,' the smaller one said. 'My name is Lola, and I'm Bilbo's new sister. My leg was crushed in an accident and then the vet removed it.'

'And my name is Louie—I'm Bob's brother. An autorickshaw ran over my leg ...' He held up his front paw, which dangled uselessly. '... But they've let me keep it for now.'

'But,' Shingmo said, confused, 'but how can you run so fast with just three legs?'

AAAWOOO!

'Easily.' Lola laughed. 'Come, race me!' She leapt into the water neatly and started running.

Shingmo hesitated for a moment, then she ran: she ran as fast as she could—until she heard her heart in her ears; she ran faster, until she heard the wind whistling—but she couldn't beat Lola.

'Come on,' Lola shouted, 'you can do it. Don't give up, brown girl!'

'My name is Shingmo! And I give up!' Shingmo panted, slowed down and stopped. 'You win,' she said. 'You deserve to be the fastest.'

'Thanks,' Lola said shyly. 'But don't worry, I'll let you win someday!'

The two girls laughed, and they ran back to the rest of the gang.

Louie was digging a hole near Bob. He flung sand on the beagle's head, and Bob snarled at him.

'If I'm given a bath, I will eat your dinner today and tomorrow!' he growled.

'Lola, can we go home now? I need to teach you how to sit still!' Bilbo called out.

'So shall we meet here again tomorrow?' Lola asked.

'Yes, I can't wait,' Shingmo said, and she ran to tell Puchu she had made a new friend.

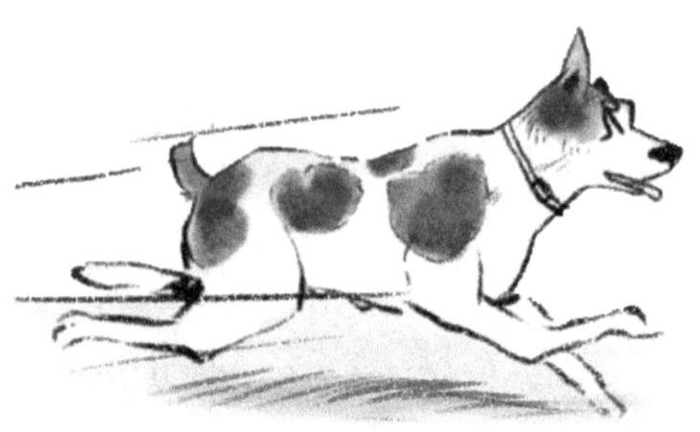

Puchu Wears a Cone

'I had the best time, Puchu! Lola—that's the fast one—has only three legs, but how she runs! Come race with me; I'll pretend to be Lola, and you can be Shingmo, okay?' Shingmo spoke breathlessly. Puchu did not reply.

'What happened, Puchu?' Shingmo asked. 'And why are you panting?'

'I feel ill, Shingmo. Let's go home, okay?' Puchu said, and walked slowly towards Mother. They went home, and Puchu went straight to bed, refusing dinner.

The moment Mother saw Puchu the next morning, she knew she was unwell. She took her straight to the vet.

'She's been a little lethargic for a few days, doctor,' Mother said, worried. 'I thought it was the heat. What's happened to her?'

'I suspect she has an infection. Can you hold her? I want to scan her abdomen,' the vet said.

So Mother held Puchu's neck and praised her and sang to her, and the vet quickly examined her belly.

'Ah,' the vet said, 'ah. I think we'd better operate and remove her uterus. It's not looking good!'

Mother was in tears. 'An operation! That's horrible!' she said, stroking Puchu's head and neck and kissing her. 'Can't we avoid it?'

'No, that will be dangerous. She won't feel a thing anyway,' the vet promised. 'We'll be giving her anaesthesia.'

So they fixed the surgery in two days' time.

Mother, Father and Girl fussed over Puchu. They fretted about the surgery. They took Shingmo for small walks, so she didn't have time to meet Lola, but she was too anxious to meet friends anyway. She just told Thin quickly that Puchu was not well. She'd be back soon, she promised.

Puchu knew something was up when Girl made her wear a plastic cone around her neck, as practice. 'Teach her to put that on; wearing it, she won't be able to bite on her bandages or open her sutures,' the vet had said.

'I'm sure Puchu won't do that,' Mother said.

'Lots of dogs do; no harm in making her wear one,' the vet replied firmly.

And so Puchu walked around with a plastic cone, frightening Shingmo: she thought the plastic had eaten her friend's face, and she tried to fight it and free Puchu.

'This is going to be fun,' the family thought. 'We're going to have one recovering dog and one loony dog!'

But it turned out their fears were unnecessary.

On the day of the surgery, Mother and Father took Puchu to the vet. Shingmo stayed home with Girl. She walked to the door and back a hundred times, as if she knew Puchu would be back soon.

And she was, in five hours.

'How did it go?' Girl asked.

Mother carried Puchu wrapped in a blanket, still groggy, the plastic cone around her face. 'They removed her uterus successfully; she'll be okay. She needs medicines for ten days and plenty of rest.'

'I hope Shingmo won't bite her sutures!' Father said.

'I don't think so. Just look at them!' Mother said, teary-eyed.

For Shingmo had quietly climbed on the bed and curled up next to Puchu.

And for the rest of the day, she did not leave her sister's side.

'Shingmo, you're a darling!' Mother said, and Father hugged her, and Girl brought her treats.

Puchu barely moved, and she slept all night. When Shingmo came back from her morning walk, she ran to greet her.

'How are you, Puchu?' she asked, and licked her nose.

Puchu was better. She sat up a little, ate some mushy food and swallowed her medicines. Mother told her 'what a good girl Puchu is', and she felt happy.

Shingmo brought a chew toy. 'Would you like to chew?' she asked Puchu.

'No, but why don't you tell me what you saw on the beach? I miss my morning walk!'

And so Shingmo became Puchu's eyes and ears for ten days. She came back running from her walks and told Puchu everything.

'This evening, there was a very big crowd. So many people came to bathe on the beach. The waves were so high, Puchu'—Shingmo pointed to the ceiling—'and the police came and blew whistles and asked people to move back, until slowly the beach emptied; there were only waves and Mother and all of us dogs. And we were allowed to stay because we played on the sand and we didn't go into the water, not once!'

The next morning, Shingmo told Puchu about the pop-up salons on the beach—men getting haircuts next to a wall, a small mirror hung from a tree and an old thermocol box for a bench.

'And while the haircuts happen on one side, massages are given on the other side; it's a whole new business, Puchu. The oils smell like flowers—you know the ones the women sell from baskets? The smell is the same, except these oils are sticky, and they taste yucky. I know because Orange tasted some once, and he said he'd never ever want a massage; he was happy being a dog!'

Shingmo also entertained Puchu with gossip.

'Oh, and Puchu, all the girls on the beach got their uteruses removed. They called them their 'lady bits' and said they didn't miss them at all. They went for the operation in a van, and afterwards they stayed in a cage for some days, and now they have a scar on their tummies. They can never have babies, they said, but that's it,' she explained.

'Thug got hauled off to the police station! He bit an important dog—you know, one of the bushy ones that come with lots of walkers?—and their humans complained. Now the police don't know what to do with him! Krya says they wanted to fine him, but as if he has money!' she giggled.

In three days' time, Puchu felt much better. Her cone was removed, and she began to walk around the house, and sat and saw the beach from the lawn.

'You can start coming for walks very soon.' Shingmo ran around Puchu happily. 'And you can watch me race Lola!'

'Who comes first now?' Puchu asked.

'Oh, Lola always does, but I don't mind,' Shingmo said good-naturedly.

'You're a good girl, Shingmo,' Puchu said, sitting down next to her. 'And you know what? You're the best sister!'

'Thank you, Puchu.' Shingmo blushed. She felt as if she had been given a present.

'And as a treat,' Puchu continued, 'I'm going to let you shout at all the cats in the next house. There goes one—come on, do your best!'

And Shingmo went 'rooaarrrrrrrrr, wowowowow', while Puchu looked on proudly.

CHAPTER FOURTEEN

I Am Thug

ook, I should be charging you for listening to my story—it's so fantastic. I'm only telling it to you for free because I like you. You'll make a good disciple, an excellent Disreputable. And when you walk around the beach, other dogs will beg your pardon, they'll drop whatever they're eating; you'll feel like a lord! Oh stop drooling at the thought—sit down and give me your ear.

Ugh, not so close. Your ear smells of dead birds. Kids these days I tell you …

When I was a pup, I didn't get to roll on dead animals. No, not even old sea creatures that live inside shells. I was raised well, you see. I lived with two very shaggy dogs, in a bungalow by the beach. They were called Hunky and Dory, and everybody loved them. They also loved me, but distantly. I didn't mind ... the boarding and lodging were excellent. Even the biscuits were first class. I dream of them sometimes.

But the good times came to an end. My family got transferred to a country far, far away. They took Hunky and Dory with them. 'This one's just a stray. We're not taking him,' they told the relocation agent. The agent felt sad for me, and he took me home. He meant well, poor thing, but there was no way he could afford to buy the kind of treats I was used to. So he gave me to a wealthy friend who could, but had no time for me. No walks, no sun, no air—it was miserable living in that flat, all alone, waiting for my human to come home, waiting all day for that one chin scratch, for my bowl of water to be filled again. For a hug.

Many days even that did not happen. He paid me no attention; he was busy, busy, busy. So I began to demand it. I jumped on him, I pulled his hand, his sleeve. I took away his phone, his wallet, his watch. It was fun, running around the house, chasing and playing. But soon, he started hitting me. 'Bad boy'—that's the only thing he called me. He told the agent I was a rogue, the agent took me back, and this time, he put me on the beach ... He said I was sure to get killed ... But look at me now: fitter than ever, loved by so many—what?

BAD BOY!

Right. You don't love me. You fear me. That's okay. The point is, I have my Disreputables around me always. That's all that matters.

I don't seem to have much luck with people. They don't enjoy my company. Some of them find me too demanding. Others think I'm ugly. I can't change my face, can I? I can't grow cute and fluffy like those small, bushy dogs they love! And when they don't like you, they call you Thug and fling things at you. Sometimes it's a chappal. Sometimes it's a stone. It hurts. And when you tell them it does—when you growl or bare your teeth—they call you a bad dog, a nasty dog, they complain about you, and pack you off to a shelter.

I'm not proud of it, but one time, I came this close to biting a human. In my defense, I felt threatened and cornered. I nipped his trouser, he screamed and a big crowd gathered. They called me a lot of awful names, the worst in many languages, and it scarred me. You know, people keep talking about this thing called kindness; they write poems and songs about it, but I haven't really seen it much …

Of course, some people are kind, but mostly, they're very, very busy. They don't have time to notice us; we're just lumps curled up on the sand. I miss chats and scratches, you know—

Yes, you can sit next to me. Yeah, scratch me there, just above my tail ... You're a good boy. I'll make you Chief Sidekick. You can howl first at the full moon. And you can get the best pickings from the big dustbin. Promise to watch over me when I sleep, will you? Hug me sometimes, I miss that ... And if you ever tell anybody all that I told you, you're in big, big trouble ...

A Storm and Some Saviours

A few weeks before the monsoon, the air became thick and sticky, like halwa. Everybody sat under the fan; people sweated profusely, dogs panted gently.

Mother sat, fanning herself furiously with a newspaper, then she wiped her forehead with her sleeve, and scolded Puchu when she found her dress covered in dog hair.

Puchu shook her head to say it wasn't her fault, but then a small cloud of fur flew. Mother glared at her. Puchu hung her head and panted some more.

'When will it rain!' Mother wailed, and Father said 'tomorrow'.

Mother scoffed.

'It's true. They're predicting a cyclone, see.' He held out his phone, and there, in big letters, she read, 'First Cyclone in Mumbai in Years'.

Nobody wanted the cyclone. But a big one was coming.

The next morning was grey. The sun went missing, and a naughty wind scattered and chased the dark clouds. The wind wandered into the house, making the curtains dance, rattling the windows panes, sending every piece of paper flying.

Puchu and Shingmo were puzzled. They hardly ever missed their walk on the beach. But mother said it was closed, that there were police and lifeguards, and they would stop them.

So the two curled up on the bed and shut their eyes.

Down by the beach, Krya and gang could not sleep. It was much too loud, wet and scary. The coconut trees swayed vigorously, dropping nuts and fronds, and sand flew around, getting into their eyes and fur.

'Big Head, go and fetch Coconut,' Krya ordered.

'You don't have to. I'm here,' Coconut said, walking up slowly.

'Krya,' he said, 'this storm is going to be brutal.'

Krya nodded. 'I know. Let's all move to high ground.' She led them up the steps towards the shops.

The first CRACK of thunder came just after the fat lightning tore up the sky.

Puchu and Shingmo were terrified, and they ran and hid behind Mother.

The dogs on the beach heard it ten times louder. Their eyes went wide with fear, they pressed their ears flat on their heads, and sat in a group and shivered.

Suddenly, Orange growled. Krya looked up. Thug was there with the Disreputables.

'Go away,' Krya snapped. 'We're not in the mood for a fight.'

'Not fighting,' Thug said brusquely. 'Our shelter's gone; the roof's blown off. Can we sit here with you?'

Krya narrowed her eyes. She didn't trust Thug.

Before she could reply, Coconut spoke. 'One wrong step, and I'll teach you,' he barked.

Thug nodded. He sat down, and the Disreputables crouched around him.

BOOM, the sky rumbled and roared, and the rain began. It came down in ropes, and soon, they could see nothing: not the lifeguards, not the policemen, not even the sea screaming and rushing up to the shore.

'It's been three hours! It shows no sign of stopping!' Mother grumbled as the rain lashed the windows.

'At least we have power,' Father said, and before he could complete the sentence, the electricity went off. The fan stopped, the house grew quiet, and the world outside went wild …

'What's that noise?' Puchu asked Shingmo, tipping her head to one side.

'Dogs. Barking. They're saying something …' Shingmo said, rushing up to the window to hear better.

'Come back, you two. Don't stand there!' Mother yelled.

But Shingmo wouldn't move.

'Puchu, something terrible is happening … we must go!' Shingmo barked.

'Are you mad? Look at the storm!' Puchu woofed back.

'There's no time; our friends need us—run!' Shingmo barked, rushing towards the front door.

Puchu followed Shingmo. Mother followed Puchu.

'Oi, you two! Go back!' She wagged a finger.

Shingmo leapt on the door.

'Ha, it's shut!' Mother said, crossing her hands and smirking.

But she was wrong. The wind had shaken the door violently, and when Shingmo leapt at it again, the bolt opened, the door swung, and the two dogs squeezed through and disappeared down the stairs.

Mother screamed. 'They've run away, they've run away!'

Father and Girl came at once, picked up the house keys and ran after the dogs.

The three stopped when they got to the bottom of the stairs. The rain was like a curtain. They could see nothing. Water swirled around their ankles. And there were no dogs around.

'They'll come back,' Mother whispered, 'won't they?' and she looked at Father and Girl.

Both nodded their heads. But they really weren't sure ...

The dogs were sure where they had to go: to the beach.

They bent their heads and ran; they slipped under the garden door—Puchu struggling a little bit, her podgy bits crushed under the grill—and landed softly on a very soggy beach.

'Quick—that way!' Shingmo yelled, pointing her nose to the left.

Puchu saw a group of dogs standing by the waves, barking.

'That's Krya and Big Head over there, and aren't those Orange and Thin?' she asked Shingmo.

'Yes, but why are they there?' Shingmo asked, her fur a deep red, drenched in the terrible rain.

Puchu shook her fur, and drops of water flew, more landing on her back.

Shingmo started running towards the gang. 'Hey!' she called out. The dogs turned to look. 'What's happening?'

'Some fools decided to go for a swim. They're drowning!' Big Head told her, craning his neck this way and that.

'Shouldn't we save them?' Shingmo asked. 'I can swim!'

'Thug's gone in,' Krya said. 'He's taken the Disreputables with him.'

'What!' Puchu asked, shocked. 'Thug?'

'I'm getting worried, Krya,' Thin said, pawing her leader. 'The waves are too high, too rough. Do you think they can bring back three boys?'

'You're right. We must all go. There's no other choice,' Krya said, and asked them to follow her. But she stopped when she reached the water's edge—the waves were angry and loud and high. They hissed and sucked and sprayed.

It would be crazy to go into that sea.

It would be cowardly not to.

Krya bent her head, took a deep breath and walked in.

'Big Head,' she yelled, 'you come to my left. Orange, you go that way. Thin, Chocolate, follow me ...' And she started swimming.

'And what about us?' Shingmo asked, but Krya was already ten feet away, a small golden head bobbing above the rolling waves.

'We didn't come all the way here to stand around,' Shingmo muttered. 'Let's go!'

And she jumped into the water, Puchu wading in after her. The rest of the pack was deep into the sea.

Thirty feet away, they found Thug and the Disreputables, struggling to hold on to three boys. They clasped their shirts in their mouth, but the waves were strong, as though they had hard muscles; they pushed the dogs away, they spun them around, they poured salty water over their heads.

Thug's eyes were bulging. His teeth were chattering. The boys had nearly fainted.

Krya took one look and decided they needed to get help. She turned around to go back to the shore. She found Shingmo right behind her.

'Go find people!' she yelled, and the little dog understood at once. She took a deep breath and began swimming, her slim legs paddling wildly, her

lungs gasping for air, crossing one agonising foot after the other. Several minutes later, she reached the shore, ran up to the lifeguards who had taken shelter behind the shops, and she barked and barked.

'What is it? What's wrong?' they asked her, wondering if the beach dogs were in trouble. They followed her in the pouring rain and the driving wind, until they reached the sea. Cupping their hands over their eyes, they squinted, and saw the dogs valiantly holding on to the boys.

They knew they had to go in. At once.

The men ran into the sea, swimming swiftly, until they reached the three boys, each held up by a few struggling dogs. They grabbed the lads by their armpits, hugged them close, and swam back clutching them. When they reached the shore, they carried them on their shoulders all the way to the shops and called for an ambulance. They didn't forget the dogs. Two men ran back, looking for them, and waited till they were safely out of the water. The dogs were exhausted—they had used every last ounce of their energy to swim, and they wearily made their way, one by one, to the shops. And while the men waited for the medical team, the dogs curled up in their spots, wet and shivering, miserable and cold.

Coconut walked up to Krya. He placed a paw on her shoulder and nudged her gently with his nose.

She looked up at him. The elderly dog licked her face gently. He was proud of her. Krya wagged her tail weakly. Shingmo curled up next to her foster mother, placed her head on Thin's plump neck, and the two were soon snoring gently. Puchu decided she'd keep watch, but in two minutes, she was asleep sitting up, her head falling, her eyes closing, and she slid down next to her friends.

Big Head and Orange went up to Thug. 'You're a hero,' they said, and Thug stood a little bit taller.

'Thanks,' he said gruffly. 'Would you like to join us here?'

And all the boys sat down together, until Chocolate came up and said she had to be a part of the group too, and they made place for her in the middle.

In two hours, the rain stopped. The clouds crossed over into the city, the waves quietened and became gentle, and Mother, Father and Girl came running to the beach.

'Puchuuuuuuu, Shingmooooo,' they cried, and the two dogs woke up with a start and ran to their family.

'We were so worried,' Mother and Father said, over and over. Girl clipped on their leashes, and they went back home to a dry house and a warm meal, while the beach dogs were in for a surprise.

They woke up and found themselves surrounded by people with raincoats and cameras and mikes.

The lifeguards had told everyone what had happened: three boys had recklessly slipped into the sea, on a beach far away, when nobody was watching. Their fun only lasted a few minutes, for a very strong current dragged them all the way to this beach, where the fierce waves tossed and terrified them. Had Thug not seen them shouting for help, they'd be dead by now. Thug had barked instructions to the Disreputables—which Shingmo had picked up with her great ears—and the whole pack had reached the boys just when they were about to drown.

'If it weren't for the dogs,' the boys' relatives said that night to the television crew, 'we would have lost our children.'

Everybody stroked the dogs' heads, and gave them biscuits and buns. The families thanked the lifeguards and the police, and they fussed over the dogs once again.

The next day, two newspapers had photographs of Krya and Thug and every dog in their gang. A movie star posted a picture on Instagram and thousands of people liked and commented on it. They said they were community dogs and real heroes. Many people turned up on the beach and took selfies with them.

'This is the good life,' Chocolate said, as someone put a garland around her neck and gave her two crunchy biscuits.

'I could get used to this too,' Thug said, as everybody took turns to shake his hand.

'Our life is not easy,' Krya said wisely, 'but maybe we're better than our friends on the streets. That life can be real mean!'

'Puppies get crushed under cars; dogs die under buses ...' Thin said, shuddering.

'Hush, not today. Right now I feel like a celebrity,' Orange said, strutting around.

'Don't let it all go to your head,' Coconut chuckled. 'You're still going to find your meals from the dustbin ...'

'Uff, you're such a bore,' Big Head said. 'Let us be happy for a day, will you?'

And the dogs went off to pose for pictures, this time with Shingmo and Puchu, and all their friends ...

CHAPTER SIXTEEN

A Cardboard Box on the Beach, Again!

Three days before the great Mumbai monsoon, a small cardboard box appeared on the beach. Krya saw it first—she scolded Orange and Big Head, she scolded Chocolate and Thin, and told them they were all completely useless.

'We just survived a storm, and now this! Another puppy will emerge, and we're sunk! And just before the rain! I can smell it; it's just over there,' she said, pointing her nose at the darkening horizon.

'But, but ...' Thin began, but Krya shushed her.

'I won't accept any excuses. What were you all doing? Shouldn't you be more vigilant?' she asked.

'But, but ...' Big Head began, and this time Krya exploded.

'What is with you lot? So much butting!' she snapped.

Orange came straight to the point. 'That's not a puppy; that's chicken.'

'What? Now they're abandoning hens?' Krya asked, her eyes bulging, her nose twitching, smelling the box. 'Hmm, yes, this smells of chicken, but, but ...'

'Yes, that's what we also said,' Thin pointed out helpfully.

'Who brought us chicken?' Krya asked us.

'It's Shingmo's beach anniversary, and we're having a party!' Orange said. 'We're going to eat nice food!'

'So why didn't you tell me this right away?' Krya asked, sitting down next to the box, guarding it.

'As if you let us,' Chocolate mumbled.

'What are we waiting for—why can't we eat? I'm hungry!' Orange begged.

'Wait for me, wait for me,' squealed Shingmo. She came bounding up, wearing a fancy red raincoat. She was taller than Puchu now, longer than her too, and her tail was thick and swishy. Her nose was black, her chin white, and she looked odd and beautiful at once. 'I need to be there; it's my party! Sing for me, everybody!'

'Shingmo, why are you wearing a raincoat? It is sunny today!' Thin asked kindly.

'My Mother's simple; she read somewhere it will rain today—she believes everything! Can't she tell it is at least three days away?' And Shingmo pointed her nose at the darkening horizon.

'Good girl,' Krya said, 'you're a proper Indie now.' She patted Shingmo's back approvingly.

'What's an Indie?' Orange asked. 'Aren't we strays?'

'Well, yes, but we're also Indies. We have a little bit of several dogs. Shingmo has some Hound—look

at her stomach arch! And Puchu, anybody can tell she's got some Terrier in her. Orange, your parents were floofy and fat, some large dog. And Chocolate has some Labrador in her—just look at how shiny her coat is!' Krya explained.

'So you remember all that I taught you!' Coconut said, walking up slowly. 'Shingmo, happy beach birthday! Now don't ask me to eat anything; I don't feel like it at all! Maybe it is time …' He sighed and sat down.

'Don't talk rot!' Krya said gruffly. Secretly, she worried about Coconut. His face had turned fully white, his joints were swollen from years of sleeping outdoors during the damp and cold months, he breathed noisily … but he was a fighter, and surely he would be around for a bit longer?

'Thank god you didn't start the party without us!' the Twins came running. 'Where's the food? Give me the food!' they clamoured.

Orange pulled a face. 'I thought I could eat Coconut's share,' he told Big Head.

'There's enough for everybody,' Shingmo said. 'Father's bringing some more stuff. I'm going for a walk. Coming, Puchu?' she called, and ran. And just as she went towards the water, a butterfly went past her nose, and Shingmo ran after it, a beautiful brown dog, in a red raincoat, chasing a blue butterfly on a warm evening …

Thin and Puchu followed her slowly.

'Is she always like this?' Thin chuckled when Shingmo bumped into the man selling paper windmills, and the two older dogs watched as the excited girl furiously licked his leg in apology, galloped again, stopped to greet the cotton candy seller, and ran ahead to meet Lola.

'Let's race!' Shingmo called out. The two young dogs ran and ran, swift as arrows, until they reached the rocks, and then they ran all the way back, and Shingmo announced, 'I won, I won.'

Lola laughed and said, yes, it was her beach anniversary and she deserved to win. Thin patted her on the back, and Puchu said, 'Let's go, little one ... don't you want to cut your cake?'

And with all her friends around her, Shingmo the seventh bit into a special dog cake. Krya and gang ate a piece each, then they ate a nice meal of rice and chicken and watched the sun set in the deep sea. And then night came to the beach, and Krya curled up behind a streetlamp, rolled herself into a tight ball, flicked her tail over her nose and slept.

Shingmo and Puchu walked up to the water and watched the dark waves, with their white lips, roll up to the shore. Mother, Father and Girl sat on the sand, waiting for the dogs. As they watched, an old, crumbling basket came riding on a tall wave.

HAPPY
BIRTHDA
SHINGMO

Shingmo barked at it and called it a Cane Monster. A small wave brought it to the shore. Shingmo ran and hid behind Puchu. 'Look, it doesn't bite,' Puchu said, tapping Cane Monster with her paws. 'Oh, I wasn't frightened at all,' Shingmo said, and walked back towards her family ...

The end

MOTHER HERE
COCONUT TREES
OLD DOGS AREA
OUR DOGGO AREA.
PIGEON AREA.
ROCKS
THIS MAP BELONGS TO SHINGMO

ROAD
CAR'S RUN HERE →
SHOPS
HUMAN'S ENTRY WAY.
YOU GET FOOD HERE
THE DISREPUTABLES' AREA
THE SEA
IT GET'S DEEPER HERE
E
W

Woof! Woof! Woof!

Puchu bounded into my life on 14 February, 2017 and changed it, forever. Shingmo came home on 17 December, 2018. The two dogs—both Indies, rescues—have been my constant companions through good days and bad. Without them, this book would never have happened. And I wouldn't have met Krya, Thin and the other beach dogs, who taught me how to love, walked with me every morning and sat by my side and watched a hundred glorious sunsets ...

Big thanks to:

My daughter Lasya, my friends R. Krithika and TP, who patiently read every version of this book; my husband, for being an amazing dog-father; my parents, for being there, always.

Vidhi Bhargava, my lovely editor, for commissioning this book, for the terrific suggestions, and for making my dream—of writing a book of dog stories—come true.

Sagar Kolwankar, for the fantastic illustrations, the exquisite details, and bringing the beach and the dogs to life.

To the dog parents—Tejas Kapadia, Michelle Kapadia, Rasika Tyagi, Tarun Tripathi and Rhythm Doshi—who gave me permission to include their pets' names and stories in this book.

To P. Sainath, Shrey Sangani, Neha Golwala, Michelle Kapadia, Srijan Mahajan and Aakanksha for their inputs with early drafts.

And to the wonderful community of animal lovers, thank you for doing all that you do. You bring so much hope and kindness to this world.

Other Red Panda Books

Thank God It's Caturday!
A Collection Of Cool Cat Stories
By Various Authors
Illustrated by Lubaina Bandukwala

Move over Friday, it's Caturday! a day to celebrate cool cats with stories by some of India's foremost children's authors.

Why Is My Hair Curly?
By Lakshmi Iyer
Illustrated by Niloufer Wadia

Why Is My Hair Curly? is a delightful celebration of curly hair and the courage it takes to be yourself. This chapter book explores genetics, family dynamics and adoption identity through a light-hearted and sunny tale.

The Crocodile Who Ate Butter Chicken for Breakfast And Other Stories
By Khyrunnisa A.
Illustrated by Meenakshi Iyer

Animals and humans of all shapes and sizes get up to odd antics in these delightful stories by bestselling children's author Khyrunnisa A. Humorous and often moving, *The Crocodile Who Ate Butter Chicken for Breakfast and Other Stories* is a rollicking read, especially for anyone who's ever loved an animal.

The red panda is a reddish brown mammal
with a long, ringed tail and a raccoon-like face.
This endangered animal is found in the forests of
eastern Himalayas and is the state animal
of Sikkim. Also called firefox, the cat-sized animal
is largely herbivores but also eats insects. The red
panda uses its bushy tail to balance and wrap
it around its body to stay warm in the
chilly mountains. A victim of deforestation, there
are less than 10,000 animals remaining in the wild.

www.ingramcontent.com/pod-product-compliance
Lightning Source LLC
Chambersburg PA
CBHW070528160726
48003CB00004B/1732